ADVENTURE IN
MOROCCO

Makanaka's World: Adventure in Morocco
MakanakasWorld.com

Copyright © 2018 by Christine Mapondera-Talley

Illustrated by *Anil Tortop*
Designed by *Ozan Tortop*
TadaaBook.com

Edited by *Christine Van Zandt*
Write-for-Success.com

All rights reserved. No part of this book may be reproduced or transmitted in any form or by any means, electronic or mechanical, including photocopying, recording, or by any information storage and retrieval system, without permission from the publisher. For more information contact Global Kid House LLC, 1020 Park Drive #594, Flossmoor, IL 60422.

First Edition, 2018
Library of Congress Control Number: 2017916830

ISBN: 978-0-9965511-2-0

To the JTs in my life, I love you. —C.M.-T.

Makanaka (Maa-kah-NAH-kah) loved her wrist gadget—a transmitter.

"Oh my noodles, Fari (FAH-ree), there's a new message!"

"Stupendous!" squawked Fari.

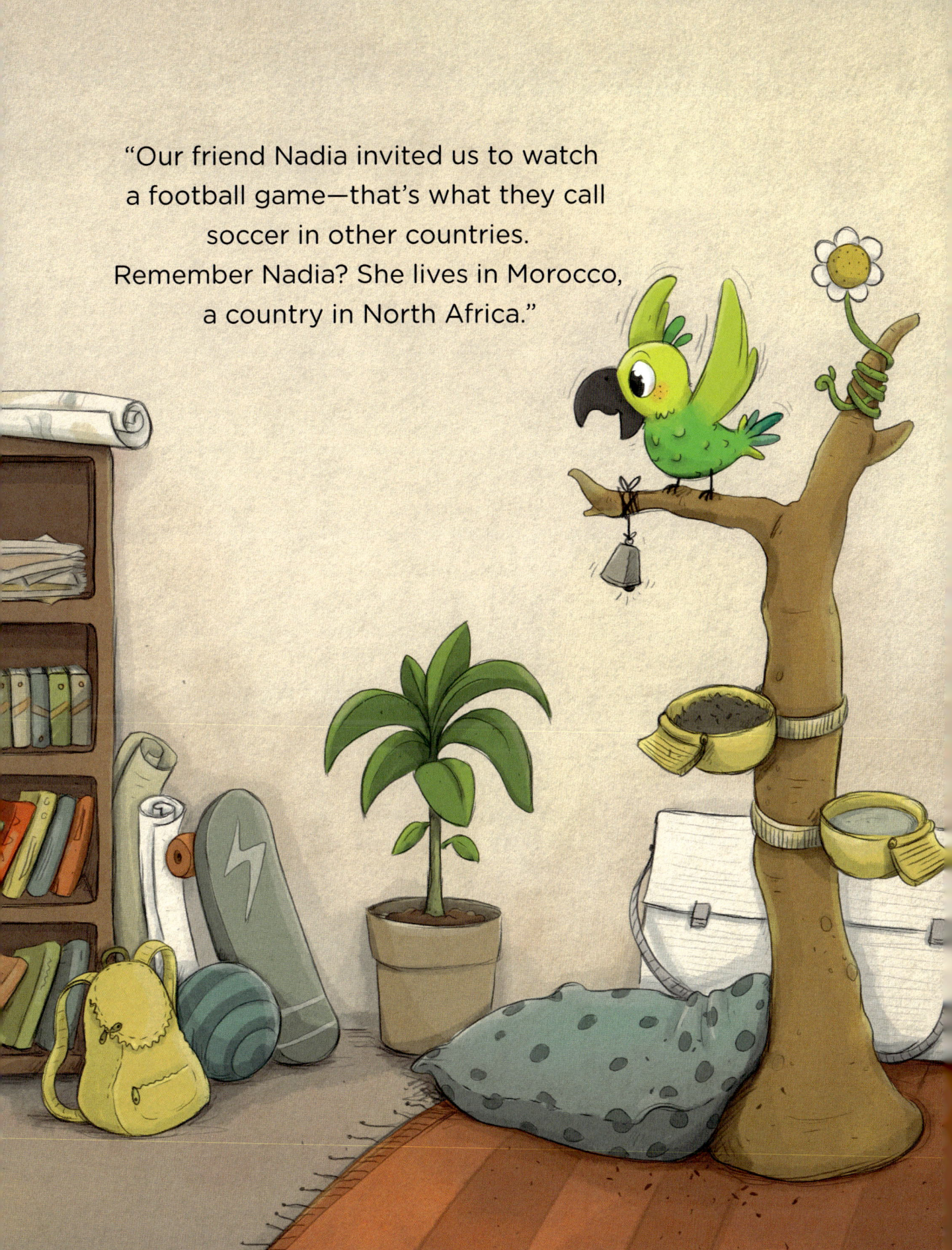

"Our friend Nadia invited us to watch a football game—that's what they call soccer in other countries. Remember Nadia? She lives in Morocco, a country in North Africa."

Makanaka was bubbling with excitement.

"Fari, ready to transform?"

"Engine on…all set!" replied the parrot.

"To Casablanca, Morocco!" shouted Makanaka.

"There's Marrakesh." Makanaka pointed.
"We had such fun exploring the *souks* (sooks) last time!"

"Yes, it was a colorful treasure island!" exclaimed Fari.

"The big city of Casablanca is close now," said Makanaka.

Makanaka greeted the other girl in Arabic.
"*Salam* (SE-lam), Nadia."

"Salam, Makanaka," replied Nadia.

Makanaka peered closely at her friend.
"Is something wrong?"

Nadia nodded. "We can't play today's game.
Our ball disappeared!"

Makanaka gasped. "Oh no! That's terrible!"

"The other kids will be here soon. This is the last game before school starts," said Nadia.

"We've got to figure out who took it! Are there any clues?" asked Makanaka.

"I noticed big shoe prints near the storage shed," said another teammate.

"Let's follow them!" suggested Makanaka.

Nadia led the way.
The girls followed the prints
to a very busy street
by the Hassan II Mosque,
but then they lost the trail.

Nadia was puzzled.

"Maybe that was a wrong clue," said Makanaka. "We should ask the people who live behind the field if they've seen your ball. What color is it?"

"Red with green stars," said Nadia.

The girls split into two groups.

They knocked on door...

after door...

after door.

Until finally...

an elderly woman pointed. "A red *kura* (KU-raa) with green stars rolled that way."

The kids reached a dead end.
Nadia's ball wasn't there.

But Makanaka heard a noise from a nearby bush.
She walked over to check it out.

"Oh my noodles!" Makanaka exclaimed.
"Quick! Everyone, come here!"

"That's my puppy, Bibi!" said Nadia. "I forgot how much she loves to play with balls. Awesome detective work, Makanaka!"

"Game on!" cried Fari.

The other kids arrived and the game started.

They kicked, headed, and passed the ball. Makanaka and Fari cheered as Nadia scored the winning goal for her team.

"Yay!"

"Hooray!"

When the game was over, Makanaka and Fari
joined everyone for a treat.
Nadia's mom served mint tea and
Moroccan cookies called *ghribas* (GRI-bahs).

"This is the best day ever!" exclaimed Makanaka.

It was time for Makanaka and Fari to go home.

"I hope I'm not too heavy to fly," moaned Fari.

"*Beslama* (be-sle-mah)," called Makanaka to her friends as she waved goodbye.

"I think there's another adventure ahead," said Makanaka.

"Stupendous!" squawked Fari.

A MINI TOUR OF MOROCCO

Morocco is a country in North Africa. People in Morocco speak Arabic, Amazigh, and French. Mint tea is a very popular drink.

CASABLANCA
(CA-SA-BLAN-CA)
This is the largest city in Morocco.

CHEFCHAOUEN
(SHAF-SHAWAN)
Often called Blue City because of its blue buildings and doors.

Glossary of Words

Souk: Marketplace

Salam: Means peace,
but also used as a general greeting

Kura: Ball

Ghriba: A type of cookie

Beslama: Goodbye

Our mission at **Global Kidz House** is, to elevate and celebrate the diversity of Africa and the African diaspora. Join us for fun activities, free downloads, book events and discount offers.

globalkidzhouse.com

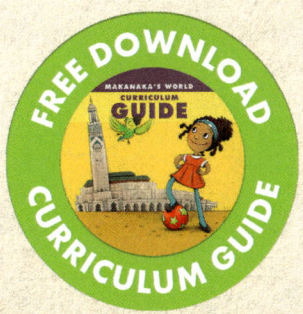

About the Author

Christine Mapondera-Talley is the author of Makanaka's World, a picture book series designed to teach children about world cultures, geography and languages in a fun and engaging way. Christine was born in Chinhoyi, Zimbabwe, and now resides in Chicago with her husband and two children. Growing up bilingual gives Christine a unique perspective to help children learn about the globe.

About the Illustrator

Anil Tortop was born and raised in Turkey. She moved to Australia in early 2011 and has been trying to get used to the local eight-legged house intruders and slithering visitors to her garden ever since. Anil also works as a character and concept designer. Nowadays, she lives with her husband in Brisbane. In their small home studio, they play *'Children's Booksmithing'* together.

Book reviews are important.
Please consider leaving a review
on Amazon.com and Goodreads.com.
Thank you!

Made in the USA
Columbia, SC
27 December 2020